INTRO DUCTION

Who Wrote 1 John?

The authorship of this epistle is attributed to John, the disciple of Jesus. Beyond 1st John, he also wrote 2nd and 3rd John as well as the Gospel of John and Revelation. There should be a level of excitement and anticipation knowing who wrote this letter because we are reading somebody's words who had a first-hand account of life with Jesus.

1 John 1:1 says, "That which was from the beginning, which we have heard, which we have seen with our eyes, which we have looked at and our hands have touched—this we proclaim concerning the Word of life." He was an eyewitness to the life of Jesus. He heard, had seen, and touched the Word of life itself. This alone is of great importance as we consider the credibility of the words that are written in this letter.

Most scholars believe that 1 John was written towards the end of John's life near the city of Ephesus. Although the letter is not addressed to a specific church or city, it is believed that John had pastoral oversight of the greater area. This is why in Revelation he addresses the early chapters to the 7 churches in that region. This letter had widespread distribution because the themes found in it had greater application than for a single person, church, city, or even period of time. John's words throughout this letter fight to secure truth and love as central elements of the Christian faith. As he writes to re-align the focus of the early church, his words hold just as much weight for the modern church today.

What Led John to Write 1 John?

One of the main causes for this letter to be written was the rise in false teaching. In the decades following the death and resurrection of Jesus, Christianity began to explode. In "The Rise of Christianity," Rodney Starks writes that towards the end of the first century, when 1st John was written, there were upwards of ten thousand Christians. Because of this quick growth it became increasingly difficult to monitor and hold accountable all of the teaching that was taking place. That's why so much of Paul, Peter and John's writings are dealing with false teaching.

The rise in this false teaching led to a second leading theme. As false teachers denied the lordship of Christ, they also made claims that it was possible to live without sin. This meant there was no need for the Christian doctrine of forgiveness. They moved so far outside of orthodox teaching that they abandoned the notion of love for one another. John is dismayed by this false teaching (1 John 2:26) and because of this, the call to love others becomes a central theme.

What Are Some Key Takeaways?
In this letter, you'll discover John emphatically reinforcing core elements of the Christian faith:
1. The Lordship of Jesus.
2. Holy Living.
3. Christlike Love for One Another.
4. Sound Doctrine.

GET THE MOST OUT OF THIS STUDY

COMMUNITY
SERVE DAY
SIGN UP

LIFE GROUP
SIGN UP

SIGN UP
TO
GET
BAPTIZED

CHILD
DEDICATIONS
SIGN UP

VOLUNTEER
AT TRUNK
OR TREAT

ONE DAY OFFERING

One of the core values at Lake City is generosity! We have been blessed to be a blessing! One of the ways this is expressed is through our annual "One Day Offering" where we give a day's wage as we partner with Convoy of Hope to provide children and families with nutritious food, safe drinking water, and much more. Half of what is received is given to Convoy of Hope. The other half is equally divided between other community partners and global partners to financially support the important work they are doing. In short, every single penny of what is given leaves the four walls of Lake City to make an impact in our city, across our region, and around the world in the name of Jesus!

This year, we are focusing our efforts toward the following initiatives:

1. Evangelism

2. Human Trafficking

3. At risk kids

4. Addiction recovery

5. Basic human needs

The "One Day Offering" will take place on Sunday, November 19th. Please prayerfully consider how the Lord would stir your heart toward generosity on this special day!

TABLE OF

CONTENTS

WEEK I

KNOWING JESUS AND MAKING HIM KNOWN

MITCH ELLITHORPE - EXECUTIVE PASTOR

1 John 1:1-4 (NIV)

That which was from the beginning, which we have heard, which we have seen with our eyes, which we have looked at and our hands have touched—this we proclaim concerning the Word of life. 2 The life appeared; we have seen it and testify to it, and we proclaim to you the eternal life, which was with the Father and has appeared to us. 3 We proclaim to you what we have seen and heard, so that you also may have fellowship with us. And our fellowship is with the Father and with his Son, Jesus Christ. 4 We write this to make our joy complete.

1 JOHN 1:1-4 (NIV)

READ

In the opening verses of 1 John, we read about the importance of sharing what we have personally experienced in our relationship with Jesus. John declares that he has heard, seen, and touched Jesus, and he shares his experiences so that others may experience the same thing!

Not only does sharing our personal experiences with Jesus strengthen our faith, but our testimonies have the power to inspire, encourage, and bring others into fellowship with Jesus. When we share about what Jesus has done in our life, we participate in the fulfillment of His plan and experience joy as a result! As we reflect on John's words today, may we be stirred to boldly proclaim the 'Word of Life.' Let us be people of hope in a hurting world, pointing people to the transforming power of following Jesus.

That which was from the beginning, which we have heard, which we have seen with our eyes, which we have looked at and our hands have touched—this we proclaim concerning the Word of life. 2 The life appeared; we have seen it and testify to it, and we proclaim to you the eternal life, which was with the Father and has appeared to us. 3 We proclaim to you what we have seen and heard, so that you also may have fellowship with us. And our fellowship is with the Father and with his Son, Jesus Christ.

REFLECT

Spend some time in quiet reflection.

How has your life been transformed? How have you seen the power of God at work in your life? What 'good news' do you have to share?

Read Acts 4:1-20 for further reflection.

1 JOHN 1:3 (NIV)   … our fellowship is with the Father and with his Son, Jesus Christ.

READ

Like any relationship we have with those around us, our relationship with God requires intentionality to be healthy. Just like our relationships with friends and family, if we aren't being intentional, those relationships will become distant or even fade away. So how do we cultivate a deeper fellowship with Jesus? It's all about establishing intentional rhythms of spiritual growth!

These Rhythms include:

Engaging with God - As we engage with God through prayer, the study of His Word, worshiping Him by the way we live our lives, and repenting of our sin when we fall short, we come to know Him in a greater way and are transformed as a result.

Living in Community – Scripture gives us many examples of how important it is to our spiritual health for us to be in relationship with others. Examples like bearing one another's burdens, encouraging one another, and holding one another accountable. Nobody thrives in isolation, we need community!

Serving with Purpose – Serving with purpose is not just a task but a deep commitment to love and serve others as Christ did. As we put others needs ahead of our own, we implement what Jesus modeled for us during His life on Earth. By understanding our unique gifts and purpose through serving, we can make a lasting impact in the lives of others to fulfill His mission!

Giving Generously – We are blessed to be a blessing! God has provided for us in so many aspects of our lives. The spiritual act of giving what God has given us not only strengthens our faith, but it also opens a doorway to bless those whom the Holy Spirit leads us to.

Multiplication – As we grow as disciples who are engaged in the mission of Jesus, an important piece of our growth is to make more disciples. Jesus said in Matthew 28:19 that we are to make disciples who are fully devoted to Him. It is our responsibility as Christ Followers to lead people to a relationship with Jesus and engage them on this same mission.

This isn't a check list to get into heaven, but more of a self-check to see how we are working towards and cultivating a fully devoted relationship with Jesus. If we are intentionally working on each of these areas of our faith journey, God will continue to grow us into all that He intends us to be.

REFLECT

Are these rhythms a regular part of your life? What can you implement in your life this week?

II

1 JOHN 1:3a (NIV)   We proclaim to you
what we have seen and
heard, so that you also
may have fellowship
with us.

READ

Have you ever felt distanced from others in the church? Maybe you've heard others share stories of how God has changed their lives, or maybe people keep referencing shared experiences and it leaves you feeling disconnected from what others have been involved with.

That feeling isn't unique, it's actually something we all wrestle with at different times and it's something that's being addressed in this passage. John is sharing about the most important events of his life, "what we have seen and heard", this is in reference to the incredible things Jesus had done.

John's goal here is to help others come to a complete understanding of how important these events were for them too. This way new believers would be able to join into the fellowship of the church and recognize the value they bring to the community. John used a specific word to communicate the importance of this, Koinónia.

Koinónia is the Greek word for fellowship. It's primarily used to communicate partnership (Philippians 1:5), communion (1 Corinthians 10:16), and spiritual fellowship (2 Corinthians 13:14); John also uses it 4 times between verses 3-7. When we see John use this word it should evoke an understanding of active involvement on our part. This is not a passive community but one that needs each of us to take hold of the calling we've received (Ephesians 4:1) and actively work towards building true Koinónia.

REFLECT

How have you been a part of the Koinónia of the church?

What are ways that you can take part in building the Koinónia of the church?

What could your life look like in 5 years if you had Koinónia with those in the church?

1 JOHN 1:2 (NIV)   The life appeared; we have seen it and testify to it, and we proclaim to you the eternal life, which was with the Father and has appeared to us.

READ

Being married to a person who is deeply creative and artistic has its challenges when I struggle to draw stick figures. My wife, Natalie, has the incredible ability to create and design. To be honest, it genuinely amazes me how she can see things in her mind and then translate it into physical form. The tension, however, lies in the moments where she will try to describe to me shapes, colors, dimensions, and other design elements of something, and my very uncreative brain simply can't picture it. I lack the ability to describe things unless I have seen them in front of me first.

Part of the reason the early church grew so explosively is the fact that when authors like John testify about Christ, they were testifying about a person and friend that they had physically seen raised from the dead. They weren't trying to describe something they had only imagined. John says in verse 2, "The life appeared, we have seen it and testify to it." "The life" is, of course, in reference to Jesus. While we have never spent a night around a campfire with Jesus, have we as his disciples not experienced the very real life-changing presence of God? Have we not experienced his hope? Have we not experienced his very real love and grace for us?

Matthew 28:19-20 is known as the great commission, and it is where Jesus sends the disciples, and now us, with the mission of creating disciples through all the earth. If we are to create disciples that are fully devoted followers of Christ who are obedient to his truth, being transformed by his spirit, and engaged on his mission, it begins with us sharing the very real truth that the life and hope of Jesus isn't just something we have fabricated and are now trying to describe, but rather we are testifying of transformation that we have personally experienced.

REFLECT

What are the tangible ways that God has changed your life?

What opportunities do you have to testify about the ways that Christ has changed your life?

Read Matthew 28:16-20 and 1 Peter 3:15-16 for further reflection.

WRITTEN BY
LINDSAY ELLITHORPE

1 JOHN 1:4 (NIV)   We write this to make our joy complete.

READ

During our years as youth pastors, Mitch and I got the privilege of seeing numerous students take their first step of faith. It was always an exciting and joyful moment, but some were a little more memorable than others. About ten years ago, I had a really special group of high school girls that I was discipling. Every week we got together for bible study at our home. One of the girls, Danni, often came early or stayed late and always showed up with a list of questions for me. One night Danni decided that she was ready to trust Jesus with her life and prayed right there at our kitchen table for her salvation. The next day after school, her and I went and bought her first bible. Those days and the following months and years after were really special times in Danni's life as she grew to know God and eventually lead most of her family to Him as well. But, those moments also marked me and my faith in a way that I'll never forget.

I think that's what John is referring to in 1 John 1:4 when he says he is writing this letter to the believers to "make our joy complete." Although it can be intimidating or nerve-wracking at times, there's something foundational that happens when we share our personal faith with someone, and it then becomes their personal faith as well. John makes it clear that we don't need to feel the pressure to live the perfect life or never mess up, but instead we can be quick to make God the hero of our story and celebrate all He has done for us. Genuine life change is always the greatest witness to God's power at work within us. Talk about joy complete! Today may we look for opportunities to share the joy we've been given in Christ with the people God has put in our lives!

REFLECT

Does the idea of sharing your faith make you feel joyful or fearful? If it sparks fear, why do you think that is?

Take some time talking to God about the fears you have about sharing your faith. Ask Him for opportunities to make your joy complete!

WEEK 2

LIVING IN THE LIGHT
MITCH ELLITHORPE - EXECUTIVE PASTOR

1 John 1:5 – 2:2 (NIV)
This is the message we have heard from him and declare to you: God is light; in him there is no darkness at all. 6 If we claim to have fellowship with him and yet walk in the darkness, we lie and do not live out the truth. 7 But if we walk in the light, as he is in the light, we have fellowship with one another, and the blood of Jesus, his Son, purifies us from all sin. 8 If we claim to be without sin, we deceive ourselves and the truth is not in us. 9 If we confess our sins, he is faithful and just and will forgive us our sins and purify us from all unrighteousness. 10 If we claim we have not sinned, we make him out to be a liar and his word is not in us.

2:1My dear children, I write this to you so that you will not sin. But if anybody does sin, we have an advocate with the Father—Jesus Christ, the Righteous One. 2 He is the atoning sacrifice for our sins, and not only for ours but also for the sins of the whole world.

1 JOHN 1:5 (NIV)

This is the message we have heard from him and declare to you: God is light; in him there is no darkness at all.

READ

If you have spent any amount of time around Christ-followers, chances are you have heard Jesus referred to as "the light." Objectively, describing anything else as "the light" outside of flashlights, candles, and lamps seems a little strange. It doesn't make sense to describe things incapable of illumination with the word "light," yet the Bible often refers to Jesus as "the light."

In John 1:5, we notice that it says, "God is light." Notice it doesn't say, "God provides light" or that, "God is a light." This isn't to say that God isn't a lighthouse to those who are lost, or that God doesn't guide our steps through the darkness with the light of his word. These things are true; Psalms 119:15 says that his word is a lamp unto our feet. With that in mind, saying that God is light has deeper implications than him just being a source of light for our lives.

By saying that God is light, this passage illustrates the fact that God is the very embodiment of perfect holiness, and where he is, darkness cannot exist. He is not just a light in the middle of darkness, he is the light that removes darkness, which has practical implications for those that follow him. Christ, through his death and resurrection, has made us pure and given us new life. While it is true that we will never be perfect, as we begin to walk in the light of Christ, we recognize that there are dark places in our life that no longer can exist. This is because the light of Christ has revealed to us the gap between his righteousness and our imperfections.

As he reveals those things, we find hope in the fact that we are loved and forgiven through the blood of one who has no darkness in Him, and that the Holy Spirit is always with us in the process of becoming more Christ-like.

REFLECT

What does it mean for Christ to be the light?

What are the dark areas of your life that God has pointed out to you?

What are the practical steps that you can take to walk away from those things?

How can you lean into the Holy Spirit when tempted to walk in darkness instead of light?

Read John 8:12 and 1 Thessalonians 5:4-5 for further reflection.

1 JOHN 1:6 (NIV)   If we claim to have fellowship with him and yet walk in the darkness, we lie and do not live out the truth.

READ

Darkness is not a thing by itself. It is only the absence of something else—namely light. Walking in darkness indicates that you are walking alone. The Light is no longer with you. Why would this be when God promises to never leave or forsake us (Psalm 94:14)? If you are walking in darkness, is it possible that it is you who left?

When my youngest son, Ryan, was about four years old, I took him to Toys R Us. We were walking together through the aisles, looking at all the amazing toys (Ryan's perspective) and noticing there wasn't much we could afford (my perspective). There came a point where there was a small crowd in a constricted area. To get where we wanted to go, we would have to navigate our way through the people and around a couple of shelves. Ryan was right next to me as I began to maneuver through the people. But when I got to the other side of the crowd and through the maze of shelves, I discovered I was alone. Ryan was nowhere to be found.

At first, I thought it would be easy to find him since he was right behind me only moments ago. But after five minutes of frantic searching, I couldn't find him. I was just about to go to the front of the store to find a manager when I turned a corner and found Ryan. He was standing next to a shelf, head down, and crying. I embraced him immediately, relieved that my lost son was found.

At some point in Ryan's journey, he found himself walking alone. He did the only thing his four-year-old brain knew to do—he wept. But we have another step we can take if we find ourselves walking in darkness. It's called repentance.

One of the reasons it took so long to find Ryan was that I was looking for him, but he stopped looking for me. Grief overtook him, and he put his head down. What if he had lifted his head and looked for me too? He would have discovered that he wasn't alone after all—that his father was right there.

If you find yourself walking in darkness...walking alone...lift up your head. Return to the Light of the World. He's ready to embrace you.

REFLECT

Are you walking in the light in every area of your life? Are there areas that need the light shined on them?

If you need to repent in one of these areas and turn back to God, what's holding you back?

If you are ready to repent, who can you contact and share this news with?

Read John 3:19-21, 2 Corinthians 6:14, Ephesians 5:8, and Isaiah 2:5 for further reflection.

19

1 JOHN 2:1-2 (NIV)   My dear children, I write this to you so that you will not sin. But if anybody does sin, we have an advocate with the Father—Jesus Christ, the Righteous One. 2 He is the atoning sacrifice for our sins, and not only for ours but also for the sins of the whole world.

READ

During my junior year of high school, I was taking a test called the PSAT. This test is used to identify and award merit scholarships for college, so the stakes were high. It's a long test that takes multiple hours and my brain was starting to run out of gas. I glanced over my shoulder to see what time it was and, almost instantly, I was called to the front of the room by the proctor of the test. She informed me (in front of all my classmates) that I was cheating and had disqualified myself from completing the test. I tried to explain that I was looking at the clock, not at the paper of the person next to me but it didn't matter. I was dismissed.

I called my dad to pick me up and explained what had happened. I remember him asking me something to the effect of, "Be honest with me. Did you cheat?" I emphatically stated that I did not. When he arrived at the school to pick me up, he had me wait in the car and he went inside to chat with the proctor on my behalf. However, despite his efforts and regardless of the fact that none of my answers matched the paper I was supposedly cheating off of, I still wasn't allowed to finish. It didn't matter to me though. My dad had advocated for me. And it meant the world.

John writes that Jesus advocates for us. This means that he comes to our aid and pleads our case. He stands between our repentant hearts and the righteous Law of God. He stands in the gap when we sin saying, "My sacrifice is sufficient for the debt their sin has created. I've paid their penalty so they can be pronounced, 'not guilty.'"

On what authority does he say this? On the authority of his atoning sacrifice on the cross. The word atone means, 'to make amends' or 'to appease' or 'to reconcile.' Through the finished work of Jesus on the cross, we can be reconciled to God and experience total forgiveness. This reality is available to anyone who turns to him in faith for salvation. That's good news!

(By the way, I was able to retake the test and I earned one of the top scores in my class. Who presented the award to me? The proctor who kicked me out earlier that year. Poetic justice!)

REFLECT

What comes to mind as you think about Jesus as your advocate?

In what ways can you extend the forgiveness and mercy you have received through Jesus' atoning sacrifice to those around you today?

Read 2 Corinthians 5:11-21 for further reflection.

1 JOHN 2:3 (NIV) We know that we have come to know him if we keep his commands.

READ

When I was still new to coming to church and our 'zip code' was in the very back of the auditorium, Pastor Mike called for anyone who was in need of prayer to stand up. He then instructed anybody around the people who were standing to begin to pray over them. A lady right in front of me stood up and I was so uncomfortable! I knew I should pray for her but I wasn't going to. I remember thinking, "Lady, we are in the back for a reason." This poor lady stood alone right in front of me and neither I nor anyone else around her came to her rescue. While the rest of the congregation prayed over others, this woman sank into her seat and began to weep.

It's hard to admit, but sometimes I know God is calling me to do something and I just simply don't do it. But in 1 John 2:3, we learn that we can never really know God unless we are following his commandments. One thing I've learned is that God has yet to call me to do something that I regretted doing. My biggest regrets in life come from those moments I chose not to listen. Following His commandments isn't always easy but it's something you'll never regret.

REFLECT

Is there anything you've been avoiding that just might be coming from God?

We say at Lake City that a disciple is a fully devoted follower of Jesus who is obedient to His truth, being transformed by His Spirit, and engaged in His mission. How are you growing in your understanding of God's truth and the application of it to your life?

Read Psalms 119 and Matthew 22:37-39 for further reflection.

1 JOHN 2:8 (NIV)   ...the darkness is passing and the true light is already shining.

READ

When our dog, Lillie, was little, she was super anxious and would constantly whine in her cage during the night. On one particularly dark night, it was my turn to go check on Lillie. I was exhausted, a little grumpy, and too lazy to turn on the lights. On my way back to our room, tragedy struck, and Jeanna awoke to a loud yelp and found me rolling around on the bedroom floor whimpering like a little child. I had broken my pinky toe on the door frame. Because I hadn't turned on any lights, I couldn't see where I was going and my foot paid the price. I had to hobble around for the next several weeks.

When we allow ourselves to stay in darkness or linger in the shadows on the outer edges of God's light, we will find that we consistently hurt ourselves and hinder our ability to move forward in our faith journey. We are blind to the truth found in Jesus, unable to distinguish the things that bring healing and life from the things that bring death and hopelessness. However, when we abide in God's light and trust in the hope we have in Jesus, everything around us starts to become clear. We can more easily identify the path that leads to a deeper relationship with Jesus. Living in the light clearly distinguishes the things of heaven from the things of the world.

REFLECT

Take some time to pray and journal, focusing on asking yourself this question: Where in God's light am I abiding? In the center? Off to the side? In the darkness?

What is hindering your ability to draw closer in God's light?

What are some steps you can take to remove these hindrances?

Read Psalm 18:28-30, John 1:1-18, Ephesians 6:10-20 for further reflection.

WEEK 3

HEALTHY RELATIONSHIPS
ANDREW TOLSON- FAMILY LIFE PASTOR

1 John 2:9-11 (NIV)
Anyone who claims to be in the light but hates a brother or sister is still in the darkness. 10 Anyone who loves their brother and sister lives in the light, and there is nothing in them to make them stumble. 11 But anyone who hates a brother or sister is in the darkness and walks around in the darkness. They do not know where they are going, because the darkness has blinded them.

WRITTEN BY
MITCH ELLITHORPE

1 JOHN 2:9 (NIV)   Anyone who claims to be in the light but hates a brother or sister is still in the darkness.

READ

Hatred is an intense dislike or ill will toward another. It doesn't often appear in our life instantaneously, instead, it's something that festers and grows over time. Hatred is rarely born out of a single offense. It's usually the result of many unresolved issues that pile up over time fueled by our own resentment, jealousy, insecurity, and unforgiveness. Hatred breeds division, bitterness, and a disregard for the inherent worth and value of people made in the image of God. Hatred shows its ugly face in our life in many ways: hurtful words, judgmental attitudes, harboring grudges, slander, and gossip just to name a few.

Given the fact that we're imperfect people in constant contact with other imperfect people, the chances that offenses will occur and the potential for hatred to emerge hovers right around 100%. This is why it's so important for us to examine our hearts before the Lord and ask, "Do I have any hatred in my heart?" This question may be uncomfortable, and it may reveal some areas of our life that we'd rather leave alone, but it's necessary for our spiritual growth and maturity. 1 John 2:9 goes so far as to say that if we harbor hatred in our heart we are living in darkness. Hatred is incompatible with the way of Jesus. We must be willing to confront the darkness within us and allow God's light to expose and transform it.

REFLECT

Is there anybody that sparks a flood of intense negative emotions just by seeing them or bringing them to mind? Ask the Lord to empower you by His Holy Spirit to begin the process of forgiving them.

Reflect on the forgiveness and grace you have received from Jesus. How can this help you forgive others?

Looking for a book on forgiveness? I recommend 'Total Forgiveness' by R.T. Kendall!

Read Ephesians 4:31-32, Proverbs 10:12, and Matthew 18:15-35 for further reflection.

1 JOHN 2:10 (NIV) Anyone who loves their brother and sister lives in the light, and there is nothing in them to make them stumble.

READ

Love is an interesting word. For as long as I can recall, love has been described by some to be an emotion and, by others, a choice. But what if it is both? What if love starts as a choice and leads to the emotion that we can sometimes feel? Feelings like joy, compassion, gratitude, or even security.

A few years ago, one of my kids was talking about how they "loved" someone. I responded to them and said, "what do you think love is?" Thinking they were going to give me some fluffy answer like, "It's that warm and fuzzy feeling you get when you're around them," I sat back and waited for my chance to be the smart dad and teach them about what love really is! To my surprise, they said to me, "Love is putting the other person's needs ahead of your own." I was stunned! Not only is that a great answer, but that was the exact answer I was going to give!

Showing true love to others means putting their needs and best interests ahead of our own. That doesn't mean that we give in to everything the other person wants, or live life as a pushover. It means we always have their best interests in mind. Sometimes that looks like telling someone a hard truth that they need to hear and other times it means to sit in silence with someone as they grieve a loss.

When we live a life of love, scripture tells us that there is nothing in us to make us stumble. This means that when we truly, and I mean truly, put others' well-being and needs ahead of our own, it has many positive effects on our lives. It affects not only the recipient of love, but our own physical and mental state. Medical studies have shown that being loving towards others lowers your blood pressure, decreases anxiety, and even lengthens your life expectancy! It's like God designed us to be loving! When we live a life with others' needs first, it helps us to align our hearts to the will of God.

REFLECT

Get practical. What does it look like today to put the needs and interests of others before your own?

Read John 13:34 and 1 Peter 4:8 for further reflection.

1 JOHN 2:10-11 (NIV) Anyone who loves their brother and sister lives in the light…11But anyone who hates a brother or sister is in the darkness…

READ

There's no question that relationships can be complicated, messy, imperfect, and quite frankly- hard on so many different levels. That is something the entirety of humanity will have in common- navigating relationships with each other. What does the Bible have to say about our relationships with others?

We were made for relationships. Being relational beings is woven into the very fabric of who God has created us to be. This is because God himself is relational. We see throughout scripture, spanning all the way back to creation that God, by nature, is relational; one God, three persons- Father, Son, and Holy Spirit. The Bible also says we were made "imago dei" -in the image of God (Genesis 1:26-27). The implication of this is that it's at the core of who we are to be relational with God AND with others.

Earlier in our study we read 1 John 1:6-7 which says, "If we claim to have fellowship with him and yet walk in the darkness, we lie and do not live out the truth. 7 But if we walk in the light, as he is in the light, we have fellowship with one another, and the blood of Jesus, his Son, purifies us from all sin."

The passage we're studying today is a continuation of that thought and it really brings the practical implication of our relationships with others into the picture. John is saying that how we love others indicates if we are living in the light. Our relationships with others reveal the reality of our relationship with God.

The love we are called to have for others is to reflect the love we have received from Christ. So I find encouragement in this- we can allow the love that we show others to be simply an overflow of the love we have received ourselves. Let that be an encouragement to you as well in reading this. God has been so kind to us, and we can let our lives be an outpouring of that kindness in how we love others.

REFLECT

In what areas of your relationships with others can you look more like Jesus?

Who do you need to forgive? Who do you need to seek forgiveness from?

Read Genesis 1:26-27 and Matthew 22:34-40 for further reflection.

1 JOHN 2:11b (NIV) They do not know where they are going, because the darkness has blinded them.

READ

I'll admit it, I've been unforgiving before. I'll probably find myself being unforgiving in the future too. It's something we all struggle with from time to time and it never has a positive or healthy outcome. In fact, Matthew 6:14-15 tells us that if we cannot forgive, we cannot be forgiven by our Heavenly Father. Holding unforgiveness in our heart only leads to hate, bitterness, and a life that is full of darkness. Many times, in my experiences with families navigating relational issues, the root of the problem is that one person did something wrong and the other person can't forgive them for it. So instead, they choose to block that person from their life out of principle. The problem is, the only thing that is really happening is more darkness enters the situation instead of the healing that God desires.

As we consider forgiveness, it's important to remember what forgiveness is not. Forgiveness is not minimizing what happened. Forgiveness is not an immediate restoration of trust. Forgiveness is not making yourself vulnerable again to their behavior. Forgiveness is not reconciliation. Here's what forgiveness is: it's a conscious decision to voluntarily release feelings of resentment, anger, and the desire for revenge toward the one who hurt you or broke your trust. The Greek word for forgiveness is 'apheimi' and it means: "to let go; to release; to keep no longer."
So how do we overcome unforgiveness? Although it's simple, it may be the hardest thing you'll ever have to overcome. We have to acknowledge, understand and choose.

Acknowledge – acknowledge the feelings of pain and hurt that someone caused you. This might even require some help from a counselor.

Understand – Understand that if I stay in a state of unforgiveness, it will only affect me and no one else. There is no worse prison on this earth than the prison of an unforgiving heart.

Choose – Choose to release feelings of resentment, anger, and the desire for revenge with the help of the Holy Spirit.

REFLECT

Read Matthew 6:14-15 for further reflection.

29

1 JOHN 1:3b (NIV)   … our fellowship is with the Father and with his Son, Jesus Christ.

READ

I love team-based games. Anything that requires collaboration and joint effort to get the job done, I'm all about. What I find amazing is that it doesn't matter that everyone is so different. Despite differences in age, physical appearance, background, etc., the team sets that all aside. Even if there is some disagreement in the execution of certain tasks, everyone is unified with one goal in mind: to win. That singular purpose bonds the entire team and pushes aside preferences so that the mission can be accomplished.

The same can be said about the church. We all have different likes and dislikes, philosophies of ministry, and even different beliefs on how to execute those philosophies. Some churches use only an organ for worship, while others have an entire band. There might even be differences in how we do communion or baptisms. However, we are all unified by one thing: Jesus. He is what binds us together and helps us to look past our differences. 2 Corinthians 3:18 tells us that we as believers are transforming into the likeness of Jesus. That means His passions become our passions, His mission becomes our mission, and ultimately His heart becomes our heart. So, if we are all striving to become the same person, it stands to reason that our hearts would look the same. There will still be differences, but the parts that truly matter are as one. By placing Jesus at the core of who we are, we resist the temptations of division, which help to promote spiritual maturity both individually and as a whole. And it is only with this unity that we are able to carry out Jesus' mission for us: make disciples of all nations, baptizing them in the Father, Son, and Holy Spirit, and teaching them to obey His commands. This is why one of our core values at Lake City is unity! We are healthiest and most effective when we're "together!"

REFLECT

Think of a time when you had a disagreement with a fellow believer. Was Jesus' heart at the center of that conflict? How could you have shifted the conversation to unify despite some differences in beliefs?

What are some areas in your own life that are not in alignment with Jesus' heart that can be causing disunity among those at church?

Ask the Spirit to reveal those areas and to guide you in taking steps to bring your heart in alignment.

Read Ephesians 4:1-16, 2 Corinthians 3:18, John 13:35, and Acts 5:32-37 for further reflection.

WEEK 4

LIVING WITH ETERNAL PERSPECTIVE

MITCH ELLITHORPE - EXECUTIVE PASTOR

1 John 2:15-17 (NIV)
Do not love the world or anything in the world. If anyone loves the world, love for the Father[a] is not in them. 16 For everything in the world—the lust of the flesh, the lust of the eyes, and the pride of life—comes not from the Father but from the world. 17 The world and its desires pass away, but whoever does the will of God lives forever.

1 JOHN 2:15 (NIV) Do not love the world or anything in the world. If anyone loves the world, love for the Father is not in them.

READ

I have been a Christian for most of my life, and I have read this verse many times. Whenever I read it, I find myself thinking, "Obviously! That is an easy one. Of course I don't love the world or the things it offers me. I don't: (insert list of "worldy" things I don't do)." But when I take a closer look, I realize that isn't entirely true. It's easy to love the world, and I am not immune to that. The worst part is, we can get caught up in this without even knowing it.

We live in a world that centers on comparison. Comparison is the antithesis of what God wants for us. I would argue that comparison keeps us from God's best for our life. How often do we find ourselves looking at our friends or acquaintances and wishing we had what they had? How often are we on social media wishing we could be on that vacation, wearing the newest fashion, or driving the newest car? Maybe for you, it revolves more around your children. Are they in the best school? Are they on the best sports team? Maybe it is where you live or what your house looks like. Whatever it is, we all can fall into loving worldly things. Look at your calendar and your bank account. Those two things will tell you a lot about what you love and value. Worldly things pull our attention from God. When our lives are centered around Jesus and our love for Him, it leaves no room for anything that opposes or rivals who He is and what He calls us to do.

REFLECT

What "comparison traps" do you find yourself falling into?

What does how you spend your time and resources reveal about the focus of your attention, affection, priorities, and values?

Read James 4:4 and Romans 12:2 for further reflection.

READ

One of the biggest movies of 2022 was Top Gun: Maverick. It was an action-packed movie with all of the right points of nostalgia thrown in. It also ended up raking in almost 1.5 billion dollars globally. The crazy thing is that it's a sequel to a movie that originally came out the year I was born: 1986.

Even though there were 36 years between these two films, there was a feeling as if everyone remembered what made the first film so iconic. Everything from "Danger Zone" playing in the background to the intense dog fights. These were the exact callbacks the second film capitalized on.

Right here in this verse, John is doing a similar thing, he's calling back to something the church would have been very aware of, even though it was written between 30-40 years prior.

In Galatians 5:19-21, Paul writes, "The acts of the flesh are obvious: sexual immorality, impurity, and debauchery; 20 idolatry and witch-craft; hatred, discord, jealousy, fits of rage, selfish ambition, dissen-sions, factions 21 and envy; drunkenness, orgies, and the like".

I. Howard Marshall, a New Testament scholar, believes that John is being intentional with his words here in verse 16. John believes the church should look different than the world so he calls back to lan-guage Paul used when he also encouraged the church to look differ-ent than the world.

Although decades separated them and centuries separate us from them, the command remains the same. We are to look different than the world around us, we are to be aware of the desire for the lust of the flesh and we are to work towards abiding in Christ.

REFLECT

How does "the lust of the flesh" disguise itself when trying to invade your life?

What can you do to live differently in a world that welcomes these de-sires?

Read Galatians 5:22-24 to see the opposite of living to the flesh.

35

READ

In the Bible, lust is defined as "sinful longing." The first example we see in the Bible of someone "lusting with their eyes" is in Genesis. Adam and Eve lived in perfect unity with God in the Garden. They had no reason to long for anything apart from God because God had provided them with everything they needed to have a perfect life with Him. In the midst of that perfection, the serpent approached Eve and with cunning words began to entice her to disobey God's instructions to not eat from one specific tree in the garden. After her conversation with the serpent, Genesis 3:6 says, "The woman saw that the tree's fruit was good to eat and pleasing to look at." When Eve looked at the fruit and saw it was pleasing to look at, it indicated a change in her heart and mind. She began taking it upon herself to decide right and wrong and longed for something that was not God's will for her life. As you continue to read the story it is clear the consequences of that longing. Sin entered the world and the relationship between God and his creation was broken.

The good news is that God fixed what was broken, reconciling us to Himself through the death and resurrection of Jesus. Now, as disciples of Jesus, we are called to live our lives as new creations, obedient to God's will. We should no longer long for things that are against God and his will for our lives. This includes the things we see. In a world full of things that can capture our attention and visually entice us, we have to be aware of what our eyes are longing for. If they are longing for things that please us but are in contradiction with God's will then we have a bigger problem happening inside our hearts and minds.

REFLECT

Read Genesis 3:1-6. Take a moment for reflection and examination. What things "look good" to you that don't line up with God's will for your life?

The lust of the eyes is a window to what is happening in our hearts and minds. What do your actions in life indicate your heart and mind are focused on?

Read Colossians 3:1-17 for a comparison of love for God and love for the world.

READ

Most of us would go to the ends of the earth for our kids' happiness. To make sure they have everything they want and experience the places that can bring joy to their lives. I can get into the routine of wanting to make sure my kids have the right outfits for school so they fit in, obsess over the vacation we should take, and then post about all of it on social media so everyone can see it and see what a super amazing mom I am! It can almost become the motivating center of our purpose. Why? What is this pull we have to be the best and have the best and then show it off?

Scripture tells us that "pull" is love for the world as expressed by the "pride of life." Simply put, the pride of life is wanting to appear important. Here's what we have to understand: When we follow what our sin nature lusts for we end up far from God and the plan He has for our lives. How do we overcome this? Well, by continuously developing a deeper relationship with God! We've read earlier that it's our fellowship with God that enables us to gain victory over the schemes of the evil one and the temptations our sin nature is drawn to.

REFLECT

So far this week we've talked about the lust of the flesh, the lust of the eyes, and the pride of life. Where is your biggest struggle right now? Take a moment to ask God to empower you and transform you so you can experience victory.

What is a practical reminder you can give yourself to reorient your thinking when you feel yourself being pulled into the temptation to appear important?

Read Luke 12:15 for further reflection.

The world and its desires pass away, but whoever does the will of God lives forever.

READ

There's a reason that the book of 1 John speaks so much about relationships. It's because relationships are the only thing in our lives that do not pass away. Everything else we hold dear—our jobs, our houses, our cars, our phones, the computer I'm writing this devotional on—they all pass away. They will either get replaced, wear out, turn to rust, or become obsolete. And in the end, it all gives way to a "new heaven and a new earth" (2 Peter 3:13).

But not relationships. Relationships last forever.

So, what is the will of God and how can we know that we are doing it? 2 John 5 says, "I am not writing you a new command but one we have had from the beginning. I ask that we love one another." Again, it's not a new command but an old one. From the beginning, God has been calling us to love one another. What are the Ten Commandments but a simple guide to loving God and loving one another? What is the Mosaic Law but a way for a community to love God and love one another? Jesus' Sermon on the Mount does not do away with the laws that came before. Rather, it calls us to a higher standard of loving God and loving one another.

God is calling this body of believers to see something greater than the desires of this world. We can give ourselves to the fleeting desires of our flesh, or we can give ourselves to cultivating relationships that last for eternity.

REFLECT

Which desires of this world are taking up your time, energy, and focus? How are those desires coming between you and healthy relationships with others?

What do your calendar and bank statement say about your priorities? Do they align with your desire to do the will of God?

Think about one relationship you have that needs your attention right now. Pray and seek God's guidance on how to go about cultivating that relationship.

Read Hebrews 12:27, Matthew 12:50, Romans 13:14, and Proverbs 27:20 for further reflection.

WEEK 5

REMAINING IN THE TRUTH

MITCH ELLITHORPE - EXECUTIVE PASTOR

1 John 2:18-29 (NIV)

Dear children, this is the last hour; and as you have heard that the antichrist is coming, even now many antichrists have come. This is how we know it is the last hour. 19 They went out from us, but they did not really belong to us. For if they had belonged to us, they would have remained with us; but their going showed that none of them belonged to us. 20 But you have an anointing from the Holy One, and all of you know the truth.[a] 21 I do not write to you because you do not know the truth, but because you do know it and because no lie comes from the truth. 22 Who is the liar? It is whoever denies that Jesus is the Christ. Such a person is the antichrist—denying the Father and the Son. 23 No one who denies the Son has the Father; whoever acknowledges the Son has the Father also. 24 As for you, see that what you have heard from the beginning remains in you. If it does, you also will remain in the Son and in the Father. 25 And this is what he promised us—eternal life. 26 I am writing these things to you about those who are trying to lead you astray. 27 As for you, the anointing you received from him remains in you, and you do not need anyone to teach you. But as his anointing teaches you about all things and as that anointing is real, not counterfeit—just as it has taught you, remain in him. 28 And now, dear children, continue in him, so that when he appears we may be confident and unashamed before him at his coming. 29 If you know that he is righteous, you know that everyone who does what is right has been born of him.

WRITTEN BY
ANDREW TOLSON

READ

1 JOHN 2:18 (NIV)

Dear children, this is the last hour; and as you have heard that the antichrist is coming, even now many antichrists have come.

If you've spent any amount of time in church culture these last few decades, you're probably familiar with the Left Behind franchise. This was a series of best-selling fictional books based on the end of the world. They used pieces of scripture to help weave a fear-based narrative about what happens to those who are "Left Behind" after the rapture. Although being strictly fiction, these books had a lasting impact on people's eschatology. (The word eschatology comes from a combination of Greek words meaning "the study of last things.")

The Antichrist became a compelling bad guy to sell books but that was never the intention of our first-century author. John's goal in this letter is to combat false teachers. As you read in the opening section of this devotional, there was a rise in false teachers and John is very explicit in his condemnation for these individuals. He even goes so far as to say they embody the spirit of the antichrist (1 John 4:3).

So, for John, the antichrists were those denying the lordship of Jesus.

When you remove the lordship of Jesus you remove God's eternal love for His creation and also Jesus' ability to be the fulfillment of every Old Testament prophecy as the one who would be the final payment for our sins. John believed those who taught this line of thinking were antichrists because what they proclaimed was antithetical to the gospel itself.

In Matthew 24:24 Jesus said, "For false messiahs and false prophets will appear and perform great signs and wonders to deceive, if possible, even the elect." John was mindful of what was taking place and enthusiastically brought it to light using similar language to what Jesus did in referencing "false messiahs," these were antichrists.

REFLECT

How does this understanding of 'antichrist' compare to maybe your previous understanding?

How can you be diligent in being aware of false teachers?

Looking for a book on this topic? I recommend "Revelation for the Rest of Us" by Scot McKnight!

1 JOHN 2:20 (NIV)   But you have an anointing from the Holy One, and all of you know the truth.

READ

What is the anointing of the Holy Spirit? How does He "guide us into all truth?" (John 16:13) To be honest, I've always had a hard time personally resonating with this idea of "anointing." However, as I've studied more about it, I've seen how anointing is a rich and beautiful theme woven throughout the entire narrative of the Bible from the garden of Eden, to the coming of Christ, and is still relevant today in the life of every believer. In the Old Testament, we read of Kings and priests and even places being anointed with oil, as to demonstrate them being set apart for God's sovereign purposes. In the New Testament, we read of Jesus Christ (Christ meaning 'anointed one') who was fully God and fully human, coming to earth for the purpose of restoring fallen creation and fully bridge the gap that sin had created between God and His people.

In 1 John 2:20, we read that now all believers have the anointing of the Holy Spirit. Meaning that God has chosen each of us to dwell within and partner with to bring about His will here on earth. How amazing! It's also important to note that in John's day, there were false teachers claiming they had a special anointing that made them "true Christians" and gave them superior knowledge. So, in this passage, John is reminding the believers that they already have the anointing of God's own Spirit who guides them to Jesus, who is called the Truth (John 16:13), and helps them to discern God's will and His love for them. We may feel insufficient sometimes in being able to discern truth and stand up against the lies of the enemy, but be encouraged today that you have all that you need through the Holy Spirit living within you and God has chosen YOU and set you apart to accomplish His sovereign purpose.

REFLECT

How can you lean into the Holy Spirit's leading this week?

In your own words, how would you describe the truth of the Gospel? (Spend time asking the Lord to reveal it to you in a greater way.)

1 JOHN 2:21 (NIV) I do not write to you because you do not know the truth, but because you do know it and because no lie comes from the truth.

READ

A few years back my son discovered the world of internet shopping! Like his daddy, he loves to find a good deal! What I forgot to teach him right away (because I am still learning this principle) is that, when you shop for deals, if something is way cheaper than it should be, there is probably a good reason for it. When it came time for him to get his first phone, he shopped online looking for the perfect one! He even got me involved and we went to meet the person we were buying the phone from. As we looked at the phone, everything seemed legitimate so we made the purchase and went on our way. When we got home, we started the process of adding service to the phone so he could use it. When the phone wouldn't allow us to, we realized the phone was stolen! I tried to contact the seller again, and to no one's surprise, the phone number no longer existed. We had been scammed.

The moral of the story? Don't buy used phones from shady teenagers in the Dairy Queen parking lot.

Since this time, I have become an over-analyzer of items that I buy. I look at every aspect of the purchase to make sure I'm getting exactly what I bargained for. I have become a student of truth about the item I am purchasing so when a fake comes my way, I can spot it immediately.

The same applies to our faith journey. It's our responsibility as disciples of Jesus to seek the truth continuously. By doing this, we become so aware of what truth looks like that we can immediately identify anything false. The only way to do this is to give ourselves to studying God's word on a regular basis. By seeking His truth through scripture, sitting under Godly teaching, and spending time in prayer we can become more aware of what truth actually looks like so we can spot a fake when it inevitably comes our way.

REFLECT

What habits do you need to develop in order to have a clearer and fuller understanding of truth?

Read Ephesians 4:11-15 for further reflection.

1 JOHN 2:24 (NIV) As for you, see that what you have heard from the beginning remains in you. If it does, you also will remain in the Son and in the Father.

READ

A saying that we are all familiar with is, "Some things just never change." Sometimes this is used to describe good moments; moments like friends reuniting and having fun just like they used to 5 years ago. Other times this phrase carries a much more negative weight because sometimes the things that "never change" are things that bring pain and sadness.

Until Jesus returns, there are two things that are unchanging. The first is the brokenness of the world. The system of ideas, values, morals, practices, and social norms that we categorize as "the world" is completely corrupted by sin and in opposition to the way of Jesus. By contrast, the second unchanging reality is the hope we have in Christ. A hope that doesn't change. A truth that isn't subjective, and a friend that will never forsake us. This is good news! This is the news that John says we should ensure remains in us. When we do, we will be settled and secure in our faith and, as a result, in our life!

The question is, what does this actually mean? Hebrews 10:23 tells us to, "hold unswervingly to the hope we profess, for he who promised is faithful." Do you hold to Christ unswervingly, or do you let go when faith is inconvenient? Is the hope you profess the hope of Jesus, or is it of your own desires? Does your deepest sense of security and stability come from external circumstances or from a living and active faith in Jesus?

REFLECT

What are the things that you often put your hope in?

What instabilities in your life do you need to give to Christ?

How can you "remain" in Christ today?

Read Romans 5:1-11 and Hebrews 10:23 for further reflection.

1 JOHN 2:27 (NIV)   ...remain in him.

READ

Water erosion is the process in which water breaks down the earth, and it's a key factor in the formation of the valleys we see around the world. Rushing streams and rivers wear away their banks and create larger valleys. The ocean waves also erode seaside cliffs, sometimes boring holes that form caves. What I find fascinating though, is that the process requires a good amount of time before we see the results. The Grand Canyon was formed through water erosion, but it has taken thousands and thousands of years to get where it is today. Water erosion takes time and persistence.

When I look at 1 John 2:27 and see the phrase, "remain in him (Christ)," I see a lot of similarities to how water breaks down the earth. In the original Greek, to remain is to, "abide, stay, reside, last, persist, and continue to live." This means that what John is saying in this passage is to not just offer a quick prayer every once in a while, he's commanding us to revolve our entire lives around Jesus. When we are at home with our families, when we are hard at work at our jobs, or even when we are studying for a test at school, we have the opportunity to remain in Jesus. Just like the consistent and tireless way water formed the Grand Canyon, remaining in Jesus is a never-ending, determined focus on Christ, and it's also the only way that we move forward in our relationship with him. According to Romans 5:3-4 and John 15:5, remaining in Jesus develops perseverance, and perseverance produces fruit. So, to break it down, we can understand the meaning and the benefit of the command to remain in Christ this way:

Commit your entire self in a way that is persistent and never-ending to Jesus. Then you will produce perseverance. And only after you develop perseverance do you begin to produce lasting fruit.

REFLECT

In what practical ways do you prioritize your relationship with Jesus in your daily life?

Are you intentional about finding time to rest and be renewed in God's presence?

Do you consistently rely on God's strength and guidance or do you tend to rely on your own strength and understanding?

Read John 15:1-11 for further reflection.

WEEK 6

LIVING AS CHILDREN OF GOD

JARED WRIGHT – YOUTH PASTOR

1 John 3:1-3 (NIV)
See what great love the Father has lavished on us, that we should
be called children of God! And that is what we are! The reason
the world does not know us is that it did not know him. 2 Dear
friends, now we are children of God, and what we will be has not yet
been made known. But we know that when Christ appears, we shall
be like him, for we shall see him as he is.3 All who have this hope in
him purify themselves, just as he is pure.

1 JOHN 3:1 (NIV) See what great love the Father has lavished on us, that we should be called children of God! And that is what we are!

READ

One of the most challenging parts of my job as a youth pastor is re-membering names. It is so challenging, but it is so important because no student wants to be greeted with "Hey............you..........." or "What's up.......bro?" Names are important, which is why in a youth ministry context, busting out the name tags every now and then is more than a little helpful.

Many of us can relate to this, that in social settings, name tags can be really helpful. Name tags help us start a conversation with a person and learn something that we will associate with their name, so that the next time that we see them they are no longer just some random person, they become, "Tim, the guy who reeeaalllllyy likes gardening." What this shows us though, is that we often associate identity with external traits like hobbies or occupations.

When it comes to my walk with Jesus, I want to see myself as, "Jared, a child of God" before I see myself as, "Jared the youth pastor," or, "Jared the guy with big insecurities." 1 John 3:1 reminds us of the fact that the defining factor of who we are lies in being children of God. This allows us to find our identity in our perfect, unchanging God and what He counts true of us instead of our shortcomings or our ev-er-changing circumstances. If our identity is in our occupation, what happens when we change jobs? If our identity is found in our role as parents or spouses, what happens when the kids graduate or our spouses inevitably frustrate us? If our identity is in our finances, what happens when financial difficulty comes along? If our identity rests in our performance or achievements, what happens when we fail?

We are called children of God. And that is what we are! Let's rest in that today.

REFLECT

Actions flow out of identity. What are the actions of someone who has found their identity in Christ? Do you see those things evident in your life?

Read 1 Peter 2:1-9 for further reflection.

1 JOHN 3:2b-3 (NIV)   But we know that when Christ appears, we shall be like him, for we shall see him as he is. 3 All who have this hope in him purify themselves, just as he is pure.

READ

I love this passage because it reminds us of the hope that we look forward to: When Jesus finally appears, we will be fully transformed into the likeness of Jesus. That means we won't have sin poisoning our bodies! We won't have to battle with it daily and struggle with its consequences. There will no longer be any anxiety or depression, no more struggling with addictions, and no more broken relationships. There will be perfect harmony of mind, body, and spirit.

But here is the amazing part: we don't have to wait to experience this freedom from sin! As we move forward in our faith journey and put the sin in us to death, the more we become like Jesus, experience true freedom, and catch a glimpse of what it will be like when Jesus returns!

So, how does this purification take place? It happens through the lifelong transformative process called sanctification. This process is initiated, sustained, and completed by the Holy Spirit as He convicts us of sin, empowers us to live in obedience, and produces spiritual fruit in us. This is why we say at Lake City that a disciple is a fully devoted follower of Jesus who is obedient to His truth, being transformed by His Spirit, and engaged in His mission!

Let's keep our eyes fixed on Jesus and lean into the transformative, purifying work the Holy Spirit desires to do within us today!

REFLECT

What are you most looking forward to when Jesus returns?

Take a moment to ask the Holy Spirit to convict you of sin. Don't view this conviction as guilt, shame, or condemnation. Instead, view it as a loving and gracious invitation to experience His best. Turn from your sin and turn toward what He is calling you to do.

Read John 14:15, 2 Corinthians 3:18, Psalm 17:15, and Romans 8 for further reflection.

1 JOHN 3:7b (NIV) The one who does what is right is righteous, just as he is righteous.

READ

When I was a teenager, my dad started a transmission shop and put me and my brother to work. I found mechanic work difficult. It didn't come easy to me at all. One day I struggled while working on a car and my dad came along. I dropped something accidentally and then announced that I was "nothing but a big klutz". My father corrected me immediately.

"No, you are not a klutz," he said. "I don't hire klutzes. You are a professional!" Something about what he said and how he said it stuck with me. I started seeing myself differently and my confidence grew. I was still an awkward teenager, but my identity was changed. He spoke something into me that day that would follow me for a lifetime.

Several years later I joined the Marines and served four years. I worked hard and took my duty seriously. Like many Marines, when I was in I had a nickname. When I got out, they gave me a plaque with my nickname engraved on it. It said, "Thank you for your service, Mr. Professional." What my father spoke into me years ago had ultimately become true.

Likewise, as followers of Christ, we exist between the "already" and the "not yet." We are already righteous because of what Christ did on the Cross. That's how the Father sees us. But we are not yet righteous in everything we do. It's as if God has spoken to us to say, "You are righteous." If we let that sink in, it can become part of our identity. But there is still work to be done. The work we do is not to become righteous—that's already been settled at the Cross. The work we do is to become, in everything we do, consistent with that identity of righteousness.

REFLECT

Do you believe what God has said of you is true? Do you believe that you are righteous in the eyes of God?

What "right" things must you do today to live up to the identity God has given you in Christ Jesus?

Read Proverbs 21:21, Genesis 15:6, 2 Corinthians 5:21, and Romans 6:18 for further reflection.

1 JOHN 3:9 (NIV)   No one who is born of God will continue to sin, because God's seed remains in them; they cannot go on sinning, because they have been born of God.

READ

Last winter, one of our daughters got in a bit of trouble at school because she was climbing on the giant snow berms that had accumulated over months of snow plowing and were strictly prohibited to kids. Linds and I asked her, "If you knew it was wrong, why did you do it?" To which she responded, "Because I had been wanting to all winter!" (Who can blame a girl?!)

Sometimes our internal desires can override what we know to be right in a situation. It's a reality we will face for the rest of our life. There won't ever be a time when we will be completely free of the tension between our tendency to sin and our desire to follow Jesus in obedience. So long as we have a sin nature and so long as we live in a fallen world, we will feel that struggle. This is especially true when it comes to deeply entrenched addictions, desires, ways of living, and ways of thinking.

So, does this mean we are not "born of God?" Absolutely not! The key in 1 John 3:9 is the words, "continue to sin" and, "go on sinning." In other words, "No one who is born of God will make sin a regular and allowable habit in their life." Why? Because the Holy Spirit dwells in us, empowering us to live in obedience to Him and turn away from sin. And when we do stumble; when the desires of our sin nature override what we know to be right, we confess our sin and receive grace from the one who is faithful and just to forgive us and cleanse us from all unrighteousness.

REFLECT

Is there a particular sin that you feel especially helpless to overcome? How can you rely on the empowerment of the Holy Spirit to a greater degree? What accountability can you establish to help you?

Read 1 Corinthians 10:13 for further reflection. What "way out" is God providing to you in the temptation you're facing?

1 JOHN 1:3b (NIV)

This is how we know what love is: Jesus Christ laid down his life for us. And we ought to lay down our lives for our brothers and sisters. 17 If anyone has material possessions and sees a brother or sister in need but has no pity on them, how can the love of God be in that person? 18 Dear children, let us not love with words or speech but with actions and in truth.

READ

When our kids were young, we lived in a close-knit neighborhood. We had neighborhood BBQ's, kids roamed from house to house, we knew each other and lived life together. One evening we had some friends over to celebrate my husband's birthday. Everyone had gone home, and we were cleaning up when our front door burst open. Our neighbor ran in letting us know our friend/neighbor had taken his kids to a very popular swimming spot on the river and drowned. Leaving a wife and two young children devastated.

As a family they attended a local church occasionally, but my friend didn't have an interest in the church. Once I invited her to an event at our church, she put her hand in my face and told me "No, that's not my thing!" Regardless of how she felt about the church we, as the church, loved this family through their grief. We helped with whatever needed to be done, without expectation of anything in return, and continued to show up again and again. Through our actions, not our words, over the years the walls came down and hearts were softened. I'm happy to say my friend is now fully committed to Christ and every part of her life has been restored.

REFLECT

Often, it's our actions, not only our words, that will draw people to Christ. How can you show Christ's love simply by showing up? I encourage you to look for ways to serve others today.

Read 1 Peter 4:10, Matthew 5:16, and Acts 20:35 for further reflection.

WEEK 7

LIVING WITH WISDOM
MITCH ELLITHORPE - EXECUTIVE PASTOR

1 John 4:1-6 (NIV)
Dear friends, do not believe every spirit, but test the spirits to see whether they are from God, because many false prophets have gone out into the world. 2 This is how you can recognize the Spirit of God: Every spirit that acknowledges that Jesus Christ has come in the flesh is from God, 3 but every spirit that does not acknowledge Jesus is not from God. This is the spirit of the antichrist, which you have heard is coming and even now is already in the world. 4 You, dear children, are from God and have overcome them, because the one who is in you is greater than the one who is in the world. 5 They are from the world and therefore speak from the viewpoint of the world, and the world listens to them. 6 We are from God, and whoever knows God listens to us; but whoever is not from God does not listen to us. This is how we recognize the Spirit of truth and the spirit of falsehood.

1 JOHN 4:1 (NIV)   Dear friends, do not believe every spirit, but test the spirits to see whether they are from God, because many false prophets have gone out into the world.

READ

Recently I had a friend reach out about a deal that was too good to pass up. We both share a love for a certain brand of shoes and he received an offer for 50% each pair purchased. After sending me the link, I looked around the site a bit and felt like something was off. I warned him that it didn't seem legit but, in his excitement, he had already bought 2 pairs. A couple weeks later the website was closed down and obviously those shoes never arrived. It reminded me of the old saying, "Don't believe everything you hear."

To answer a very serious threat of false teachers, John is calling the early church to be vigilant and aware of what is happening. "Test the spirits" is John's way of saying, "Don't believe everything you hear".

One of the more challenging tasks for the modern church is to identify false teachers and false prophets given the abundance of information and platforms to get that information out.

False teachers still prey on people's need for acceptance and identity, this is why John's call for the early church remains the same today. We must hold fast to scripture and stay committed to rooting out false teaching. John, Paul, and Peter speak at great length on this subject in their letters and provide the needed resources for testing these false voices. Some key verses are below.

REFLECT

Why do you think the early church authors wrote so adamantly against false teaching?

What are some of the false teachings you see present today?

What parts of scripture do you rely on to help test modern teachers and prophets?

Read 1 John 4:1-6, 2 Peter 2, 2 Corinthians 11:12-13 for further reflection.

1 JOHN 4:12 (NIV)   No one has ever seen God; but if we love one another, God lives in us and his love is made complete in us.

READ

The Bible is full of verses encouraging followers of Jesus to humbly serve others in love, to help those in need, and to honor God through kindness and generosity. Jesus set the standard of service for others to follow. He spent a lot of His ministry meeting practical needs. I think, if we're completely honest, most of us tend to be selfish with God's gifts and overlook opportunities to serve.

What if, instead of binging a TV show or scrolling social media, we visit someone in the hospital or take a meal to someone who's hurting? What if, instead of rushing to finish everything on our schedule, we took the time to support a single parent, befriended someone who's lonely, or simply be present with the people around us? What if, instead of waiting for God to send opportunities our way, we seek out those who may not know Him and help them see why He occupies the place of highest honor in our life.

REFLECT

Take some time to consider how your life has been blessed by others. Write down a few ways you can help others who are in need. Think of practical ways you can bless those in your neighborhood, work or school. Begin to make it a habit to bless others.

Read Philippians 2:4-8 and Matthew 20:28 for further reflection.

1 JOHN 4:15b (NIV)   God is love.

READ

The dictionary describes love as, "an intense feeling of deep affection" or, "a great interest and pleasure in doing something," which pretty much sums up the way I feel about my husband of 40 years and the San Francisco football team I have cheered on since I met him. However, as a follower of Christ, I should also reflect the kind of love that God has for His children.

The Bible says God is love. This love is more than an "intense feeling" or "great interest." It's a sacrificial love that was demonstrated when God willingly sent his son Jesus to die for the sins of all of mankind.

1 Corinthians 13 explains what this others-centered love looks like on the daily. Patient and kind. Not envious, not boastful, not proud, not rude, not self-seeking, and not easily angered. It keeps no record of wrongs and does not delight in evil but rejoices with truth. It always protects, trusts, hopes, and perseveres.

That is a tall order! I can no more manufacture patience and kindness than I can turn water into wine! And yet, I have learned that the more time I spend with Jesus, the more I resemble Him. And on the days I really seem to struggle, and my tank is running low – I realize it is partly because I have mistakenly run off without my time of refueling with Him. It is His Spirit that enables me to love as He does and be Jesus to those around me. I have a sign in my kitchen that says, "All I need is a little bit of coffee and a whole lot of Jesus," and it's true!!!

REFLECT

What's one way you can sacrificially love someone today?

Are you spending enough time with Jesus to become an accurate reflection of Him?

Read Mark 12:30-31, John 13:34-35, and 1 Corinthians 13 for further reflection.

1 JOHN 4:18 (NIV) There is no fear in love. But perfect love drives out fear, because fear has to do with punishment. The one who fears is not made perfect in love.

READ

The Greek word for "perfect" in this passage is Teleos. Another definition for teleos is "complete." Our "incomplete" way of loving often involves fear.

Author Carrie Sinclair says it this way: "Loving people is complicated. It can hurt. It is messy. Because of this, we tend to insulate ourselves from the very people who need our love. 1 John calls us to push past the fear of making mistakes or getting hurt. It calls us—Jesus' followers, God's children, and the Spirit's vessels—to love others not with 'word or tongue, but in deed and truth.'"

If you've ever been hurt before, first of all, welcome to the human race. Because you've been hurt before, it can be difficult to love without fear. That's why "perfect love drives out fear." Embrace this perfect, complete love by recognizing that this is how God loves you. Seek only to extend to others what has been freely offered to you.

REFLECT

In what ways is fear hindering you from loving more completely?

Consider how God has loved you. How has that love impacted your life? Can you imagine having that sort of impact on another person?

Read Romans 8:15, 2 Timothy 1:7, 1 Peter 2:17, and Genesis 3:10 for further reflection.

1 JOHN 4:19 (NIV)   We love because he first loved us.

READ

Loving others can be messy, demanding, and even painful at times. However, what keeps us grounded and focused on the call to love is the realization that God loved us first. His perfect love sets the example for us to follow, even when it feels challenging.

When we find ourselves wrestling with the difficulties of loving others, it is important to keep God's love at the forefront of our minds. We must continually remind ourselves of the unconditional love He has poured out upon us, despite our flaws and shortcomings. This awareness empowers us to extend love to others, even in the midst of challenging circumstances.

REFLECT

Are there any specific individuals or groups in your life that you find challenging to love? Why? What steps can you take to cultivate a heart that is more aligned with God's love for others?

How well do you love others without expectation of anything in return?

God's forgiveness is an expression of his love. Is there anybody you need to love by forgiving?

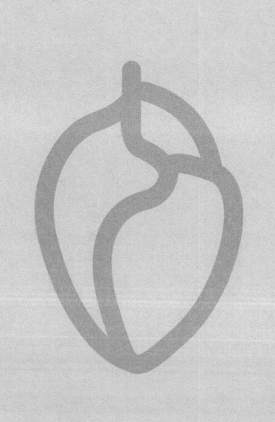

WEEK 8

GUARDING AGAINST IDOLS

KYLE PADILLA – WORSHIP PASTOR

1 John 5:21 (NIV)
Dear children, keep yourselves from idols.

1 JOHN 5:3-4 (NIV)

In fact, this is love for God: to keep his commands. And his commands are not burdensome, 4 for everyone born of God overcomes the world.

READ

When I was in high school, I played on the tennis team. On game days, we'd all come to school matching- we'd either wear our uniforms, our school colors, or sometimes we'd all coordinate dressing up formally for the day. For the most part, I loved it, except for one specific circumstance: When we had to wear our warm-up sweats. I was no fashion icon by any means, but I couldn't understand why anyone would willingly choose to wear pajamas to school all day! But when those days came, I'd throw on my grey and red sweatpants and sweatshirt every time. Why? Because it identified me as part of the team. I loved my team and coach, loved what we were accomplishing during the season, and loved being part of something bigger than myself.

I don't think God is asking us to start coordinating our outfits anytime soon, but I do think we're faced daily with a similar battle of wills- our will and desires versus God's. 1 John 5:3 speaks directly to this. Following God will always require our obedience to him. God asks us to lay down our desires and will for the greater good of a life submitted to him and his will for us. In a world that makes much of instant gratification and "following your truth," this is something we must constantly ask the Lord to help us with. When we are faced with the inevitable battle to either submit to his lordship in our lives or choose our own path, what do we do? When it's God's word up against our opinions or feelings, who wins?

I love how God knows us well enough to follow up the command in verse three with a comforting reassurance in verse four, saying, "his commands are not burdensome, for everyone born of God overcomes the world." A life submitted to God will not be without hardship, but we will experience the fulfillment of seeing a greater plan unfold that we never could have dreamt up for ourselves. May we be people who love and trust God enough to willingly obey him with our whole life!

REFLECT

Does your demonstrated pattern of behavior reveal a life submitted to the Lordship of Christ?

What areas of your life are more difficult than others to surrender to the will of God?

1 JOHN 5:7-8 (NIV) For there are three that testify: the Spirit, the water and the blood; and the three are in agreement.

READ

Despite playing golf for over 20 years, I have never recorded a hole-in-one. It's an accomplishment that cruelly alludes me. One thing is certain: a hole-in-one isn't considered official unless it can be verified by witnesses. You never believe anybody who says they aced a hole without witnesses!

Last summer I was playing by myself at Highlands Golf Course in Post Falls. I was on hole 14, a par 3. The pin was about 165 yards out. I hit a 9 iron with the hopes that it would land short and roll to the hole. (To all the non-golfers out there, I'm sorry for all the "golf-speak." To all the golfers, you're welcome.) My shot came off the club perfect with a slight fade and was tracking right at the pin. It landed softly and began rolling straight toward the hole with enough momentum to get there. As the ball got closer to the hole, I was filled with horror at the possibility that I might hit a hole-in-one by myself! I even yelled at the ball, "NO!" The ball lipped off the edge of the cup and came to rest about 3 inches away, much to my relief. Nobody believes a hole-in-one story without witnesses!

In 1 John 5, John is defending the divinity of Christ. In Jewish law it was necessary to have two or three witnesses for a case to be carried. (Deuteronomy 17:6; 19:15) In our passage today, John gives three witnesses that testify and give validity to Jesus being the Son of God:

The Spirit – The Spirit bore witness to Jesus' divinity at his baptism by descending upon him like a dove in John 1:32. The Spirit is also described as the one who "guides us into all truth" (John 16:13) and will testify about Jesus to us. (John 15:26)
The Water – The beginning of Jesus' ministry was marked by his water baptism. After he was baptized and the Spirit descended upon him, a voice from heaven said, ""This is my Son, whom I love; with him I am well pleased." (Matthew 3:17)
The Blood – The blood not only represents his humanity (being fully God and fully man; a claim many false teachers of the day denied) but, more importantly, it represents his perfect sacrifice on our behalf. He spilled his blood so that we could be forgiven and free. Ephesians 1:7-8 says, "In him we have redemption through his blood, the forgiveness of sins, in accordance with the riches of God's grace 8 that he lavished on us."

These three witnesses are in complete agreement in their testimony that Jesus is, in fact, who he claims to be. With these witnesses, we can confidently put our faith in Jesus and believe in him for salvation!

REFLECT

With this context in mind, read 1 John 5:1-12. What is God's Word speaking to you today?

Do you fully view Jesus as Lord and Savior? Or do you view him more as a moral teacher? Is today the day you put your full faith and trust in him believing him to be who he says he is?

1 JOHN 5:14-15 (NIV)

This is the confidence we have in approaching God: that if we ask anything according to his will, he hears us. 15And if we know that he hears us – whatever we ask – we know that we have what we asked of him.

READ

This verse highlights the confidence we can have in approaching God. Prayer is not simply a religious ritual, it is a powerful means of communication with our heavenly Father. We are assured in this passage that when we pray according to God's will, he hears us and responds.

I've heard this verse twisted to mean that God answers any prayer we offer. "God, I pray for a hole-in-one with witnesses!" (See yesterday's entry if that made no sense.) But that's not how God operates. God is not a genie or cosmic vending machine. He is not obligated to our every whim, craving, or desire. He is wholly committed to his perfect and sovereign purposes. Therefore, when we pray, it is important that we align and submit our hearts to his will. When we do, even when we are in the midst of uncertain circumstances, we can be certain that he hears us and will answer according to his perfect wisdom and timing.

REFLECT

Prayer is simply talking with God. How do you typically approach prayer? Is it more of a religious ritual or a genuine, two-way conversation with God?

How has God answered your prayers in the past? How have his "Yeses" and "No's" demonstrated his goodness and faithfulness in your life?

How do you align and submit your heart to God's will in prayer?

Put it into practice: Set a timer for 15 minutes and spend time approaching God with confidence in prayer!

1 JOHN 5:21 (NIV)   Dear children, keep yourself from idols.

READ

We don't craft idols to worship in our homes these days, but idolatry is no less common today than it was to John's original audience. What is modern-day idolatry?

It can be difficult to identify idol worship in our own lives. In his book "Counterfeit Gods," Tim Keller defines an idol as, "anything that is more important to you than God, anything that absorbs your heart and imagination more than God, and anything you seek to give you what only God can give." With that in mind let's look at a few ways idolatry can manifest in our lives.

Identity – When our identity (or image) is our idol, we place our highest value in the achievements we accomplish, the job we have, the following we have on social media, the clothes we wear, the car we drive, the house we live in, or the money in our bank account.
Entertainment – When entertainment (or amusement or pleasure) is our idol, we prioritize seeking activities to fill our calendar. The activities we give ourselves to may not be inherently "bad," be we'll know it's an idol when it squeezes out any time for things that Jesus prioritizes.
Comfort – When comfort is our idol, we seek ease over meaning or purpose. We pursue whatever is most convenient and instantly gratifying. When life doesn't go according to plan, we turn to whatever will allow us to not feel the pain or discomfort.

These are just a few. There are many other idols that can pop up in our life. What can you identify in your own life as an idol? What practical steps can you take to guard yourself against idolatry? Here are some questions that might help you:

REFLECT

Where do I spend my time?
Where do I spend my money?
Where do I get my joy?
What is always on my mind?

Read Exodus 20:3-6, Colossians 3:5, and John 2:8 for further reflection.

We've made it to the end of the study!

We've broken apart 1 John into 39 devotional entries, 8 Sunday messages, and 8 Life Group Discussion Guides. Take some time today to read through the book of 1 John unbroken and in its entirety. Spend time reviewing and reflecting on what you've learned throughout this study. Consider the following questions:

Are you experiencing "joy complete" in your faith? If not, what's missing?

What have been your biggest takeaways?

What steps of obedience have you taken as a result of this study?

In what ways can you more intentionally grow to become a more fully devoted follower of Jesus who is obedient to His truth, being transformed by His Spirit, and engaged in His mission?

Made in the USA
Las Vegas, NV
13 September 2023

77506382R00044